35 Cookie Recipes for Home

By: Kelly Johnson

Table of Contents

Recipes

- Matcha White Chocolate Cookies with Almond Crunch
- Lemon Blueberry Cheesecake Thumbprint Cookies
- Double Chocolate Hazelnut Cookies
- Caramel Pecan Thumbprint Cookies
- Orange Cranberry Shortbread Cookies
- **Maple Pecan Oatmeal Cookies**
- Chai Spiced Snickerdoodle Cookies
- Raspberry Almond Thumbprint Cookies
- Coconut Lime Sugar Cookies
- Pumpkin Spice Latte Cookies
- Honey Lavender Shortbread Cookies
- Dark Chocolate Mint Truffle Cookies
- Lemon Poppy Seed Ricotta Cookies
- Cinnamon Roll Sugar Cookies
- Espresso Chocolate Chunk Cookies
- Pistachio Cranberry Biscotti
- Almond Joy Cookies
- Lemon Blueberry Cheesecake Cookies
- Chocolate Hazelnut Thumbprint Cookies
- Oatmeal Raisin Cookies with Pecans
- Triple Chocolate Chip Cookies
- Peanut Butter and Jelly Thumbprint Cookies
- Snickerdoodle Cookies
- White Chocolate Cranberry Cookies
- Maple Pecan Shortbread Cookies
- Lemon Poppy Seed Cookies
- Caramel Pecan Chocolate Thumbprint Cookies

- Chai Spice Snickerdoodle Cookies
- Pistachio Cranberry Biscotti
- Raspberry Almond Thumbprint Cookies
- Raspberry Almond Thumbprint Cookies
- Chocolate Mint Sandwich Cookies
- Lemon Blueberry Cheesecake Cookies
- Pumpkin Spice Chocolate Chip Cookies
- Salted Caramel Pecan Cookies

Matcha White Chocolate Cookies with Almond Crunch

Ingredients:

For the Matcha White Chocolate Cookies:

- 1 cup unsalted butter, softened
- 1 cup granulated sugar
- 2 large eggs
- 2 teaspoons matcha powder
- 2 cups all-purpose flour
- 1/2 teaspoon baking powder
- 1/4 teaspoon salt
- 1 cup white chocolate chips
- 1/2 cup almond slices, toasted

For the Matcha Glaze:

- 1 cup powdered sugar
- 1 tablespoon matcha powder
- 2-3 tablespoons milk

Instructions:

Preheat the oven to 350°F (180°C). Line baking sheets with parchment paper.

In a large bowl, cream together the softened butter and granulated sugar until light and fluffy. Add the eggs one at a time, beating well after each addition.

In a separate bowl, sift together the matcha powder, all-purpose flour, baking powder, and salt.

Gradually add the dry ingredients to the wet ingredients, mixing until just combined. Fold in the white chocolate chips and toasted almond slices.

Drop rounded tablespoons of cookie dough onto the prepared baking sheets, spacing them about 2 inches apart.

Bake in the preheated oven for 10-12 minutes or until the edges are set and the centers are slightly soft. Remove from the oven and allow the cookies to cool on the baking sheets for 5 minutes before transferring them to a wire rack to cool completely.

While the cookies are cooling, prepare the matcha glaze. In a bowl, whisk together the powdered sugar and matcha powder. Gradually add milk until the glaze reaches a drizzling consistency.

Once the cookies are completely cooled, drizzle the matcha glaze over the top of each cookie.

Allow the glaze to set for about 30 minutes before serving.
Enjoy these delightful Matcha White Chocolate Cookies with Almond Crunch with a cup of green tea for a perfect blend of flavors and textures.

Note: Store cookies in an airtight container to maintain freshness.

Lemon Blueberry Cheesecake Thumbprint Cookies

Ingredients:

For the Cookie Dough:

- 1 cup unsalted butter, softened
- 1/2 cup granulated sugar
- 2 large egg yolks
- 1 teaspoon vanilla extract
- 2 cups all-purpose flour
- 1/4 teaspoon salt

For the Cheesecake Filling:

- 4 ounces cream cheese, softened
- 1/3 cup granulated sugar
- 1 teaspoon lemon zest
- 1 tablespoon lemon juice
- 1/2 teaspoon vanilla extract
- 1/2 cup fresh blueberries

For the Lemon Glaze:

- 1 cup powdered sugar
- 2 tablespoons lemon juice
- 1 teaspoon lemon zest

Instructions:

Preheat the oven to 350°F (180°C). Line baking sheets with parchment paper.
In a large bowl, cream together the softened butter and granulated sugar until light and fluffy. Add the egg yolks and vanilla extract, beating well.
In a separate bowl, whisk together the all-purpose flour and salt. Gradually add the dry ingredients to the wet ingredients, mixing until just combined.
Shape the cookie dough into 1-inch balls and place them on the prepared baking sheets. Make an indentation in the center of each cookie using your thumb or the back of a spoon.

In another bowl, beat together the cream cheese, granulated sugar, lemon zest, lemon juice, and vanilla extract until smooth.

Spoon a small amount of the cheesecake filling into the indentation of each cookie. Press a few fresh blueberries into the cheesecake filling.

Bake in the preheated oven for 12-15 minutes or until the edges of the cookies are golden brown.

Allow the cookies to cool on the baking sheets for 5 minutes before transferring them to a wire rack to cool completely.

In a small bowl, whisk together the powdered sugar, lemon juice, and lemon zest to make the lemon glaze.

Drizzle the lemon glaze over the cooled cookies.

Let the glaze set for about 20 minutes before serving.

These Lemon Blueberry Cheesecake Thumbprint Cookies are a delightful combination of tangy lemon, sweet blueberries, and creamy cheesecake. Enjoy!

Note: Store cookies in an airtight container in the refrigerator for longer shelf life due to the cheesecake filling.

Double Chocolate Hazelnut Cookies

Ingredients:

For the Cookie Dough:

- 1 cup unsalted butter, softened
- 1 cup granulated sugar
- 2 large eggs
- 1 teaspoon vanilla extract
- 2 cups all-purpose flour
- 1/2 cup unsweetened cocoa powder
- 1 teaspoon baking soda
- 1/4 teaspoon salt
- 1 cup semisweet chocolate chips

For the Hazelnut Filling:

- 1/2 cup hazelnut spread (e.g., Nutella)

For Topping:

- 1/4 cup chopped hazelnuts, toasted

Instructions:

Preheat the oven to 350°F (180°C). Line baking sheets with parchment paper.

In a large bowl, cream together the softened butter and granulated sugar until light and fluffy. Add the eggs one at a time, beating well after each addition. Stir in the vanilla extract.

In a separate bowl, whisk together the all-purpose flour, cocoa powder, baking soda, and salt.

Gradually add the dry ingredients to the wet ingredients, mixing until just combined. Fold in the semisweet chocolate chips.

Scoop tablespoon-sized portions of the cookie dough and flatten each portion with your palm. Place a small dollop of hazelnut spread in the center of each flattened portion.

Fold the edges of the cookie dough over the hazelnut spread, sealing it in the center.

Place the filled cookies on the prepared baking sheets, spacing them about 2 inches apart.

Bake in the preheated oven for 10-12 minutes or until the edges are set. Remove from the oven and let the cookies cool on the baking sheets for 5 minutes before transferring them to a wire rack.

While the cookies are still warm, sprinkle the chopped toasted hazelnuts on top.

Allow the cookies to cool completely before serving.

These Double Chocolate Hazelnut Cookies are a heavenly combination of rich chocolate, gooey hazelnut filling, and crunchy toasted hazelnuts. Enjoy with a glass of milk or your favorite hot beverage!

Note: Store cookies in an airtight container to preserve freshness.

Caramel Pecan Thumbprint Cookies

Ingredients:

For the Cookie Dough:

- 1 cup unsalted butter, softened
- 1/2 cup granulated sugar
- 2 large egg yolks
- 2 teaspoons vanilla extract
- 2 cups all-purpose flour
- 1/4 teaspoon salt

For the Pecan Filling:

- 1 cup pecans, finely chopped
- 1/2 cup caramel sauce

For Topping:

- 1/4 cup caramel sauce (for drizzling)
- Sea salt for sprinkling

Instructions:

Preheat the oven to 350°F (180°C). Line baking sheets with parchment paper.

In a large bowl, cream together the softened butter and granulated sugar until light and fluffy. Add the egg yolks and vanilla extract, beating well.

In a separate bowl, whisk together the all-purpose flour and salt. Gradually add the dry ingredients to the wet ingredients, mixing until just combined.

Shape the cookie dough into 1-inch balls and place them on the prepared baking sheets.

Make an indentation in the center of each cookie using your thumb or the back of a spoon.

In a small bowl, mix together the finely chopped pecans and caramel sauce.

Spoon a small amount of the pecan filling into the indentation of each cookie.

Bake in the preheated oven for 12-15 minutes or until the edges of the cookies are golden brown.

Allow the cookies to cool on the baking sheets for 5 minutes before transferring them to a wire rack.

Drizzle each cookie with caramel sauce and sprinkle a pinch of sea salt on top.

Let the cookies cool completely before serving.

These Caramel Pecan Thumbprint Cookies are a delightful blend of buttery cookies, sweet caramel, and crunchy pecans with a touch of sea salt for the perfect balance of flavors. Enjoy!

Note: Store cookies in an airtight container to maintain freshness.

Orange Cranberry Shortbread Cookies

Ingredients:

For the Shortbread Cookies:

- 1 cup unsalted butter, softened
- 1/2 cup powdered sugar
- 2 cups all-purpose flour
- 1 tablespoon orange zest
- 1/2 cup dried cranberries, chopped

For the Orange Glaze:

- 1 cup powdered sugar
- 2 tablespoons fresh orange juice
- 1 teaspoon orange zest

Instructions:

Preheat the oven to 350°F (180°C). Line baking sheets with parchment paper.

In a large bowl, cream together the softened butter and powdered sugar until light and fluffy.

Add the all-purpose flour and orange zest to the butter mixture. Mix until the dough comes together. Fold in the chopped dried cranberries.

Divide the dough in half. Shape each half into a log, about 1.5 inches in diameter. Wrap the logs in plastic wrap and chill in the refrigerator for at least 1 hour.

Slice the chilled logs into 1/4-inch thick rounds and place them on the prepared baking sheets.

Bake in the preheated oven for 10-12 minutes or until the edges of the cookies are lightly golden.

Allow the cookies to cool on the baking sheets for 5 minutes before transferring them to a wire rack to cool completely.

In a small bowl, whisk together the powdered sugar, fresh orange juice, and orange zest to make the orange glaze.

Once the cookies are completely cooled, drizzle the orange glaze over the top of each cookie.

Let the glaze set for about 20 minutes before serving.

These Orange Cranberry Shortbread Cookies are a delightful combination of buttery shortbread, tangy orange, and sweet cranberries. Enjoy with a cup of tea or coffee!

Note: Store cookies in an airtight container to maintain freshness.

Maple Pecan Oatmeal Cookies

Ingredients:

For the Cookie Dough:

- 1 cup unsalted butter, softened
- 1 cup packed brown sugar
- 2 large eggs
- 1 teaspoon vanilla extract
- 1 1/2 cups old-fashioned oats
- 1 1/2 cups all-purpose flour
- 1 teaspoon baking soda
- 1/2 teaspoon ground cinnamon
- 1/4 teaspoon salt

For the Maple Pecan Filling:

- 1 cup pecans, chopped
- 1/4 cup pure maple syrup

Instructions:

Preheat the oven to 350°F (180°C). Line baking sheets with parchment paper.
In a large bowl, cream together the softened butter and brown sugar until light and fluffy.
Add the eggs one at a time, beating well after each addition. Stir in the vanilla extract.
In a separate bowl, combine the oats, all-purpose flour, baking soda, ground cinnamon, and salt.
Gradually add the dry ingredients to the wet ingredients, mixing until just combined.
In a small saucepan, heat the chopped pecans and maple syrup over medium heat. Cook for 2-3 minutes, stirring frequently, until the pecans are coated in the maple syrup.
Fold the maple pecan mixture into the cookie dough.
Drop rounded tablespoons of cookie dough onto the prepared baking sheets, spacing them about 2 inches apart.
Bake in the preheated oven for 10-12 minutes or until the edges are golden brown.
Allow the cookies to cool on the baking sheets for 5 minutes before transferring them to a wire rack to cool completely.

These Maple Pecan Oatmeal Cookies are a delightful blend of hearty oats, rich maple flavor, and crunchy pecans. Enjoy with a glass of milk or your favorite hot beverage!

Note: Store cookies in an airtight container to preserve freshness.

Chai Spiced Snickerdoodle Cookies

Ingredients:

For the Cookie Dough:

- 1 cup unsalted butter, softened
- 1 1/2 cups granulated sugar
- 2 large eggs
- 1 teaspoon vanilla extract
- 3 cups all-purpose flour
- 1 teaspoon cream of tartar
- 1/2 teaspoon baking soda
- 1/4 teaspoon salt

For the Chai Spice Coating:

- 1/4 cup granulated sugar
- 1 teaspoon ground cinnamon
- 1/2 teaspoon ground ginger
- 1/2 teaspoon ground cardamom
- 1/4 teaspoon ground cloves
- 1/4 teaspoon ground black pepper

Instructions:

Preheat the oven to 350°F (180°C). Line baking sheets with parchment paper.
In a large bowl, cream together the softened butter and granulated sugar until light and fluffy. Add the eggs one at a time, beating well after each addition. Stir in the vanilla extract.
In a separate bowl, whisk together the all-purpose flour, cream of tartar, baking soda, and salt.
Gradually add the dry ingredients to the wet ingredients, mixing until just combined.
In a small bowl, combine the ingredients for the chai spice coating - granulated sugar, ground cinnamon, ground ginger, ground cardamom, ground cloves, and ground black pepper.
Shape the cookie dough into 1-inch balls and roll each ball in the chai spice coating, ensuring they are well coated.
Place the coated cookie balls on the prepared baking sheets, spacing them about 2 inches apart.

Bake in the preheated oven for 10-12 minutes or until the edges are set and the cookies are lightly golden.

Allow the cookies to cool on the baking sheets for 5 minutes before transferring them to a wire rack to cool completely.

These Chai Spiced Snickerdoodle Cookies offer a delightful twist on the classic snickerdoodle with the warm and aromatic flavors of chai. Enjoy with a cup of chai tea or your favorite warm beverage!

Note: Store cookies in an airtight container to maintain freshness.

Raspberry Almond Thumbprint Cookies

Ingredients:

For the Cookie Dough:

- 1 cup unsalted butter, softened
- 1/2 cup granulated sugar
- 2 large egg yolks
- 1 teaspoon almond extract
- 2 cups all-purpose flour
- 1/4 teaspoon salt

For the Raspberry Filling:

- 1/2 cup seedless raspberry jam

For the Almond Glaze:

- 1 cup powdered sugar
- 2 tablespoons milk
- 1/2 teaspoon almond extract
- Sliced almonds for garnish

Instructions:

Preheat the oven to 350°F (180°C). Line baking sheets with parchment paper.
In a large bowl, cream together the softened butter and granulated sugar until light and fluffy. Add the egg yolks and almond extract, beating well.
In a separate bowl, whisk together the all-purpose flour and salt. Gradually add the dry ingredients to the wet ingredients, mixing until just combined.
Shape the cookie dough into 1-inch balls and place them on the prepared baking sheets. Make an indentation in the center of each cookie using your thumb or the back of a spoon.
Fill each indentation with a small amount of raspberry jam.
Bake in the preheated oven for 10-12 minutes or until the edges of the cookies are lightly golden.
Allow the cookies to cool on the baking sheets for 5 minutes before transferring them to a wire rack to cool completely.
In a small bowl, whisk together the powdered sugar, milk, and almond extract to make the almond glaze.

Drizzle the almond glaze over the cooled cookies and garnish with sliced almonds. Let the glaze set for about 20 minutes before serving.

These Raspberry Almond Thumbprint Cookies are a delightful combination of buttery cookies, sweet raspberry jam, and almond glaze. Enjoy with a cup of tea or as a sweet treat any time of the day!

Note: Store cookies in an airtight container to maintain freshness.

Coconut Lime Sugar Cookies

Ingredients:

For the Cookie Dough:

- 1 cup unsalted butter, softened
- 1 cup granulated sugar
- 2 large eggs
- 1 teaspoon vanilla extract
- 2 3/4 cups all-purpose flour
- 1 teaspoon baking powder
- 1/2 teaspoon baking soda
- 1/4 teaspoon salt
- Zest of 2 limes

For the Coconut Lime Glaze:

- 2 cups powdered sugar
- 3 tablespoons coconut milk
- 1 tablespoon lime juice
- Shredded coconut for garnish

Instructions:

Preheat the oven to 350°F (180°C). Line baking sheets with parchment paper.
In a large bowl, cream together the softened butter and granulated sugar until light and fluffy. Add the eggs one at a time, beating well after each addition. Stir in the vanilla extract.
In a separate bowl, whisk together the all-purpose flour, baking powder, baking soda, and salt. Gradually add the dry ingredients to the wet ingredients, mixing until just combined.
Fold in the lime zest, ensuring it is evenly distributed throughout the cookie dough.
Drop rounded tablespoons of cookie dough onto the prepared baking sheets, spacing them about 2 inches apart.
Bake in the preheated oven for 10-12 minutes or until the edges are set and the cookies are lightly golden.
Allow the cookies to cool on the baking sheets for 5 minutes before transferring them to a wire rack to cool completely.
In a medium bowl, whisk together the powdered sugar, coconut milk, and lime juice to make the coconut lime glaze.

Once the cookies are completely cooled, drizzle the glaze over the top of each cookie and sprinkle shredded coconut on top.
Let the glaze set for about 20 minutes before serving.
These Coconut Lime Sugar Cookies offer a tropical twist with the zesty flavor of lime and the sweet coconut glaze. Enjoy these refreshing cookies with a cup of coconut milk or your favorite tropical beverage!

Note: Store cookies in an airtight container to maintain freshness.

Pumpkin Spice Latte Cookies

Ingredients:

For the Cookie Dough:

- 1 cup unsalted butter, softened
- 1 cup granulated sugar
- 2 large eggs
- 1 cup canned pumpkin puree
- 1 teaspoon vanilla extract
- 3 1/2 cups all-purpose flour
- 1 teaspoon baking powder
- 1/2 teaspoon baking soda
- 1/2 teaspoon salt
- 2 teaspoons pumpkin pie spice

For the Coffee Glaze:

- 1 cup powdered sugar
- 2 tablespoons strong brewed coffee, cooled
- 1/2 teaspoon vanilla extract
- Ground cinnamon for garnish

Instructions:

Preheat the oven to 350°F (180°C). Line baking sheets with parchment paper.
In a large bowl, cream together the softened butter and granulated sugar until light and fluffy. Add the eggs one at a time, beating well after each addition. Stir in the pumpkin puree and vanilla extract.
In a separate bowl, whisk together the all-purpose flour, baking powder, baking soda, salt, and pumpkin pie spice. Gradually add the dry ingredients to the wet ingredients, mixing until just combined.
Drop rounded tablespoons of cookie dough onto the prepared baking sheets, spacing them about 2 inches apart.
Bake in the preheated oven for 12-15 minutes or until the edges are set and the cookies are lightly golden.
Allow the cookies to cool on the baking sheets for 5 minutes before transferring them to a wire rack to cool completely.
In a small bowl, whisk together the powdered sugar, brewed coffee, and vanilla extract to make the coffee glaze.

Once the cookies are completely cooled, drizzle the coffee glaze over the top of each cookie.

Sprinkle ground cinnamon on top of the glaze for added flavor and decoration.

Let the glaze set for about 20 minutes before serving.

These Pumpkin Spice Latte Cookies capture the essence of a classic fall beverage. Enjoy the warm and cozy flavors with a cup of coffee or your favorite latte!

Note: Store cookies in an airtight container to maintain freshness.

Honey Lavender Shortbread Cookies

Ingredients:

For the Cookie Dough:

- 1 cup unsalted butter, softened
- 1/2 cup powdered sugar
- 2 tablespoons honey
- 2 teaspoons dried culinary lavender, finely chopped
- 2 cups all-purpose flour
- 1/4 teaspoon salt

For the Lavender Glaze:

- 1 cup powdered sugar
- 2 tablespoons milk
- 1/2 teaspoon dried culinary lavender, finely chopped

Instructions:

Preheat the oven to 350°F (180°C). Line baking sheets with parchment paper.
In a large bowl, cream together the softened butter, powdered sugar, and honey until light and fluffy.
Stir in the finely chopped dried lavender.
In a separate bowl, whisk together the all-purpose flour and salt. Gradually add the dry ingredients to the wet ingredients, mixing until just combined.
Shape the cookie dough into a log, about 1.5 inches in diameter. Wrap the log in plastic wrap and chill in the refrigerator for at least 1 hour.
Slice the chilled log into 1/4-inch thick rounds and place them on the prepared baking sheets.
Bake in the preheated oven for 10-12 minutes or until the edges are set and the cookies are lightly golden.
Allow the cookies to cool on the baking sheets for 5 minutes before transferring them to a wire rack to cool completely.
In a small bowl, whisk together the powdered sugar, milk, and finely chopped dried lavender to make the lavender glaze.
Once the cookies are completely cooled, drizzle the lavender glaze over the top of each cookie.
Let the glaze set for about 20 minutes before serving.

These Honey Lavender Shortbread Cookies offer a delicate balance of sweet honey and aromatic lavender. Enjoy these elegant cookies with a cup of herbal tea for a soothing treat!

Note: Store cookies in an airtight container to maintain freshness.

Dark Chocolate Mint Truffle Cookies

Ingredients:

For the Cookie Dough:

- 1 cup unsalted butter, softened
- 1 cup granulated sugar
- 2 large eggs
- 1 teaspoon peppermint extract
- 2 cups all-purpose flour
- 1/2 cup unsweetened cocoa powder
- 1/2 teaspoon baking powder
- 1/4 teaspoon salt
- 1 cup dark chocolate chips

For the Mint Truffle Filling:

- 1 cup dark chocolate chips
- 1/4 cup heavy cream
- 1/2 teaspoon peppermint extract

Instructions:

Preheat the oven to 350°F (180°C). Line baking sheets with parchment paper.
In a large bowl, cream together the softened butter and granulated sugar until light and fluffy. Add the eggs one at a time, beating well after each addition. Stir in the peppermint extract.
In a separate bowl, whisk together the all-purpose flour, cocoa powder, baking powder, and salt. Gradually add the dry ingredients to the wet ingredients, mixing until just combined.
Fold in the dark chocolate chips.
Drop rounded tablespoons of cookie dough onto the prepared baking sheets, spacing them about 2 inches apart.
Bake in the preheated oven for 10-12 minutes or until the edges are set and the cookies are slightly firm.
Allow the cookies to cool on the baking sheets for 5 minutes before transferring them to a wire rack to cool completely.
In a heatproof bowl, combine the dark chocolate chips, heavy cream, and peppermint extract for the mint truffle filling. Microwave in 20-second intervals, stirring between each, until the chocolate is melted and smooth.

Once the cookies are completely cooled, spread a teaspoon of the mint truffle filling on the bottom of one cookie and sandwich it with another.

Allow the mint truffle filling to set for about 30 minutes before serving.

These Dark Chocolate Mint Truffle Cookies are a decadent combination of rich chocolate and refreshing mint. Enjoy these indulgent treats with a cup of hot cocoa or coffee!

Note: Store cookies in an airtight container to maintain freshness.

Lemon Poppy Seed Ricotta Cookies

Ingredients:

For the Cookie Dough:

- 1 cup unsalted butter, softened
- 1 1/2 cups granulated sugar
- 2 large eggs
- 1 cup whole milk ricotta cheese
- 1 teaspoon vanilla extract
- Zest of 2 lemons
- 3 tablespoons fresh lemon juice
- 2 1/2 cups all-purpose flour
- 1 tablespoon poppy seeds
- 1 teaspoon baking powder
- 1/2 teaspoon baking soda
- 1/4 teaspoon salt

For the Lemon Glaze:

- 2 cups powdered sugar
- 3 tablespoons fresh lemon juice
- Zest of 1 lemon

Instructions:

Preheat the oven to 350°F (180°C). Line baking sheets with parchment paper.
In a large bowl, cream together the softened butter and granulated sugar until light and fluffy. Add the eggs one at a time, beating well after each addition. Stir in the ricotta cheese, vanilla extract, lemon zest, and fresh lemon juice.
In a separate bowl, whisk together the all-purpose flour, poppy seeds, baking powder, baking soda, and salt. Gradually add the dry ingredients to the wet ingredients, mixing until just combined.
Drop rounded tablespoons of cookie dough onto the prepared baking sheets, spacing them about 2 inches apart.
Bake in the preheated oven for 12-15 minutes or until the edges are set and the cookies are lightly golden.
Allow the cookies to cool on the baking sheets for 5 minutes before transferring them to a wire rack to cool completely.

In a small bowl, whisk together the powdered sugar, fresh lemon juice, and lemon zest to make the lemon glaze.

Once the cookies are completely cooled, drizzle the lemon glaze over the top of each cookie.

Let the glaze set for about 20 minutes before serving.

These Lemon Poppy Seed Ricotta Cookies offer a delightful burst of citrus flavor and a tender texture. Enjoy these sunny treats with a cup of tea or as a refreshing dessert!

Note: Store cookies in an airtight container to maintain freshness.

Cinnamon Roll Sugar Cookies

Ingredients:

For the Cookie Dough:

- 1 cup unsalted butter, softened
- 1 cup granulated sugar
- 2 large eggs
- 1 teaspoon vanilla extract
- 3 cups all-purpose flour
- 1 teaspoon baking powder
- 1/2 teaspoon baking soda
- 1/4 teaspoon salt

For the Cinnamon Filling:

- 1/2 cup unsalted butter, melted
- 1 cup brown sugar, packed
- 2 tablespoons ground cinnamon

For the Cream Cheese Glaze:

- 4 ounces cream cheese, softened
- 1/4 cup unsalted butter, softened
- 1 cup powdered sugar
- 1 teaspoon vanilla extract

Instructions:

Preheat the oven to 350°F (180°C). Line baking sheets with parchment paper.
In a large bowl, cream together the softened butter and granulated sugar until light and fluffy. Add the eggs one at a time, beating well after each addition. Stir in the vanilla extract.
In a separate bowl, whisk together the all-purpose flour, baking powder, baking soda, and salt. Gradually add the dry ingredients to the wet ingredients, mixing until just combined.
In a small bowl, mix together the melted butter, brown sugar, and ground cinnamon to create the cinnamon filling.
Roll out the cookie dough on a floured surface into a rectangle. Spread the cinnamon filling evenly over the dough.

Starting from one long edge, roll the dough into a log. Slice the log into 1/2-inch thick rounds and place them on the prepared baking sheets.

Bake in the preheated oven for 10-12 minutes or until the edges are set and the cookies are lightly golden.

Allow the cookies to cool on the baking sheets for 5 minutes before transferring them to a wire rack to cool completely.

In a medium bowl, beat together the cream cheese, softened butter, powdered sugar, and vanilla extract to make the cream cheese glaze.

Once the cookies are completely cooled, drizzle the cream cheese glaze over the top of each cookie.

Let the glaze set for about 20 minutes before serving.

These Cinnamon Roll Sugar Cookies offer the delightful taste of cinnamon rolls in a cookie form. Enjoy these sweet treats with a cup of coffee or as a delicious dessert!

Note: Store cookies in an airtight container to maintain freshness.

Espresso Chocolate Chunk Cookies

Ingredients:

For the Cookie Dough:

- 1 cup unsalted butter, softened
- 1 cup brown sugar, packed
- 1/2 cup granulated sugar
- 2 large eggs
- 2 teaspoons vanilla extract
- 2 1/4 cups all-purpose flour
- 1 teaspoon baking soda
- 1/2 teaspoon salt
- 3 tablespoons instant espresso powder
- 8 ounces dark chocolate, coarsely chopped

Instructions:

Preheat the oven to 350°F (180°C). Line baking sheets with parchment paper.
In a large bowl, cream together the softened butter, brown sugar, and granulated sugar until light and fluffy. Add the eggs one at a time, beating well after each addition. Stir in the vanilla extract.
In a separate bowl, whisk together the all-purpose flour, baking soda, salt, and instant espresso powder. Gradually add the dry ingredients to the wet ingredients, mixing until just combined.
Fold in the coarsely chopped dark chocolate.
Drop rounded tablespoons of cookie dough onto the prepared baking sheets, spacing them about 2 inches apart.
Bake in the preheated oven for 10-12 minutes or until the edges are set and the cookies are slightly soft in the center.
Allow the cookies to cool on the baking sheets for 5 minutes before transferring them to a wire rack to cool completely.
These Espresso Chocolate Chunk Cookies are a perfect combination of rich espresso flavor and decadent dark chocolate chunks. Enjoy these delightful cookies with a cup of espresso or your favorite coffee!

Note: Store cookies in an airtight container to maintain freshness.

Pistachio Cranberry Biscotti

Ingredients:

For the Biscotti Dough:

- 1/2 cup unsalted butter, softened
- 1 cup granulated sugar
- 3 large eggs
- 1 teaspoon vanilla extract
- 3 cups all-purpose flour
- 1 1/2 teaspoons baking powder
- 1/4 teaspoon salt
- 1 cup shelled pistachios, coarsely chopped
- 1 cup dried cranberries

For the Optional White Chocolate Drizzle:

- 1/2 cup white chocolate chips, melted

Instructions:

Preheat the oven to 350°F (180°C). Line a baking sheet with parchment paper.
In a large bowl, cream together the softened butter and granulated sugar until light and fluffy. Add the eggs one at a time, beating well after each addition. Stir in the vanilla extract.
In a separate bowl, whisk together the all-purpose flour, baking powder, and salt.
Gradually add the dry ingredients to the wet ingredients, mixing until just combined.
Fold in the chopped pistachios and dried cranberries.
Divide the dough in half. On the prepared baking sheet, shape each portion into a log, approximately 12 inches long and 2 inches wide.
Bake in the preheated oven for 25-30 minutes or until the logs are set and lightly golden.
Allow the logs to cool on the baking sheet for 10 minutes. Reduce the oven temperature to 325°F (160°C).
Transfer the logs to a cutting board and slice them into 1/2-inch thick diagonal slices.
Place the slices back on the baking sheet and bake for an additional 15-20 minutes, turning them halfway through, until the biscotti are crisp and golden.
Allow the biscotti to cool completely on a wire rack.
Optional: Melt the white chocolate chips and drizzle over the cooled biscotti for added sweetness.

These Pistachio Cranberry Biscotti are perfect for dipping into coffee or tea. Enjoy the delightful combination of crunchy pistachios and tart cranberries in every bite!

Note: Store biscotti in an airtight container to maintain crispness.

Almond Joy Cookies

Ingredients:

For the Cookie Dough:

- 1 cup unsalted butter, softened
- 1 cup granulated sugar
- 1 cup brown sugar, packed
- 2 large eggs
- 1 teaspoon vanilla extract
- 3 cups all-purpose flour
- 1 teaspoon baking soda
- 1/2 teaspoon baking powder
- 1/2 teaspoon salt
- 1 cup shredded coconut
- 1 cup sliced almonds, toasted
- 1 cup chocolate chips

For Topping:

- Additional sliced almonds, toasted
- Additional shredded coconut
- Melted chocolate for drizzling

Instructions:

Preheat the oven to 350°F (180°C). Line baking sheets with parchment paper.

In a large bowl, cream together the softened butter, granulated sugar, and brown sugar until light and fluffy. Add the eggs one at a time, beating well after each addition. Stir in the vanilla extract.

In a separate bowl, whisk together the all-purpose flour, baking soda, baking powder, and salt. Gradually add the dry ingredients to the wet ingredients, mixing until just combined.

Fold in the shredded coconut, toasted sliced almonds, and chocolate chips.

Drop rounded tablespoons of cookie dough onto the prepared baking sheets, spacing them about 2 inches apart.

Press additional toasted sliced almonds and shredded coconut onto the tops of each cookie.

Bake in the preheated oven for 10-12 minutes or until the edges are set and the cookies are lightly golden.

Allow the cookies to cool on the baking sheets for 5 minutes before transferring them to a wire rack to cool completely.

Once the cookies are cooled, drizzle melted chocolate over the tops.

These Almond Joy Cookies are a delightful blend of coconut, almonds, and chocolate. Enjoy these sweet treats with a glass of milk or your favorite hot beverage!

Note: Store cookies in an airtight container to maintain freshness.

Lemon Blueberry Cheesecake Cookies

Ingredients:

For the Cookie Dough:

- 1 cup unsalted butter, softened
- 1 cup granulated sugar
- 1 large egg
- 1 teaspoon vanilla extract
- Zest of 2 lemons
- 3 cups all-purpose flour
- 1/2 teaspoon baking powder
- 1/4 teaspoon salt

For the Cheesecake Filling:

- 8 ounces cream cheese, softened
- 1/2 cup granulated sugar
- 1 large egg
- 1 teaspoon lemon juice
- 1 cup fresh blueberries

For Lemon Glaze:

- 1 cup powdered sugar
- 2 tablespoons fresh lemon juice
- Zest of 1 lemon

Instructions:

Preheat the oven to 350°F (180°C). Line baking sheets with parchment paper.

In a large bowl, cream together the softened butter and granulated sugar until light and fluffy. Add the egg, vanilla extract, and lemon zest, mixing well.

In a separate bowl, whisk together the all-purpose flour, baking powder, and salt.

Gradually add the dry ingredients to the wet ingredients, mixing until just combined.

In another bowl, beat together the softened cream cheese, granulated sugar, egg, and lemon juice until smooth.

Roll tablespoon-sized portions of the cookie dough into balls and place them on the prepared baking sheets.

Make an indentation in the center of each cookie with your thumb or the back of a spoon.

Spoon a dollop of the cheesecake filling into the indentation of each cookie.

Press a few fresh blueberries into the cheesecake filling on each cookie.

Bake in the preheated oven for 12-15 minutes or until the edges are set and the cookies are lightly golden.

Allow the cookies to cool on the baking sheets for 5 minutes before transferring them to a wire rack to cool completely.

In a small bowl, whisk together the powdered sugar, fresh lemon juice, and lemon zest to make the lemon glaze.

Once the cookies are completely cooled, drizzle the lemon glaze over the top of each cookie.

These Lemon Blueberry Cheesecake Cookies are a delightful combination of tangy lemon, sweet blueberries, and creamy cheesecake. Enjoy these soft and fruity cookies as a delicious treat!

Note: Store cookies in an airtight container to maintain freshness.

Chocolate Hazelnut Thumbprint Cookies

Ingredients:

For the Cookie Dough:

- 1 cup unsalted butter, softened
- 1/2 cup granulated sugar
- 2 large egg yolks
- 2 teaspoons vanilla extract
- 2 cups all-purpose flour
- 1/4 teaspoon salt

For the Chocolate Hazelnut Filling:

- 1/2 cup chocolate hazelnut spread (such as Nutella)

For Garnish:

- Chopped hazelnuts

Instructions:

Preheat the oven to 350°F (180°C). Line baking sheets with parchment paper.

In a large bowl, cream together the softened butter and granulated sugar until light and fluffy. Add the egg yolks and vanilla extract, beating well.

In a separate bowl, whisk together the all-purpose flour and salt. Gradually add the dry ingredients to the wet ingredients, mixing until just combined.

Shape the cookie dough into 1-inch balls and place them on the prepared baking sheets.

Use your thumb or the back of a spoon to make an indentation in the center of each cookie.

Spoon a small amount of chocolate hazelnut spread into the indentation of each cookie.

Garnish each cookie with chopped hazelnuts.

Bake in the preheated oven for 10-12 minutes or until the edges are set and the cookies are lightly golden.

Allow the cookies to cool on the baking sheets for 5 minutes before transferring them to a wire rack to cool completely.

These Chocolate Hazelnut Thumbprint Cookies offer a perfect blend of buttery cookies and rich chocolate hazelnut filling. Enjoy these delightful cookies with a cup of coffee or as a sweet treat!

Note: Store cookies in an airtight container to maintain freshness.

Oatmeal Raisin Cookies with Pecans

Ingredients:

- 1 cup unsalted butter, softened
- 1 cup packed brown sugar
- 1/2 cup granulated sugar
- 2 large eggs
- 1 teaspoon vanilla extract
- 1 1/2 cups all-purpose flour
- 1 teaspoon baking soda
- 1/2 teaspoon ground cinnamon
- 1/2 teaspoon salt
- 3 cups old-fashioned oats
- 1 cup raisins
- 1 cup chopped pecans

Instructions:

Preheat the oven to 350°F (180°C). Line baking sheets with parchment paper.

In a large bowl, cream together the softened butter, brown sugar, and granulated sugar until light and fluffy. Add the eggs one at a time, beating well after each addition. Stir in the vanilla extract.

In a separate bowl, whisk together the all-purpose flour, baking soda, ground cinnamon, and salt. Gradually add the dry ingredients to the wet ingredients, mixing until just combined.

Fold in the old-fashioned oats, raisins, and chopped pecans.

Drop rounded tablespoons of cookie dough onto the prepared baking sheets, spacing them about 2 inches apart.

Bake in the preheated oven for 10-12 minutes or until the edges are set and the cookies are lightly golden.

Allow the cookies to cool on the baking sheets for 5 minutes before transferring them to a wire rack to cool completely.

These Oatmeal Raisin Cookies with Pecans are a classic and comforting treat. Enjoy the chewy texture, sweet raisins, and nutty pecans in every bite!

Note: Store cookies in an airtight container to maintain freshness.

Triple Chocolate Chip Cookies

Ingredients:

- 1 cup unsalted butter, softened
- 1 cup granulated sugar
- 1 cup packed brown sugar
- 2 large eggs
- 1 teaspoon vanilla extract
- 2 1/4 cups all-purpose flour
- 1/2 cup unsweetened cocoa powder
- 1 teaspoon baking soda
- 1/2 teaspoon salt
- 1 cup white chocolate chips
- 1 cup milk chocolate chips
- 1 cup dark chocolate chips

Instructions:

Preheat the oven to 350°F (180°C). Line baking sheets with parchment paper.

In a large bowl, cream together the softened butter, granulated sugar, and brown sugar until light and fluffy. Add the eggs one at a time, beating well after each addition. Stir in the vanilla extract.

In a separate bowl, whisk together the all-purpose flour, cocoa powder, baking soda, and salt. Gradually add the dry ingredients to the wet ingredients, mixing until just combined.

Fold in the white chocolate chips, milk chocolate chips, and dark chocolate chips.

Drop rounded tablespoons of cookie dough onto the prepared baking sheets, spacing them about 2 inches apart.

Bake in the preheated oven for 10-12 minutes or until the edges are set and the cookies are slightly soft in the center.

Allow the cookies to cool on the baking sheets for 5 minutes before transferring them to a wire rack to cool completely.

These Triple Chocolate Chip Cookies are a chocolate lover's dream with a perfect blend of white, milk, and dark chocolate chips. Enjoy these rich and indulgent cookies with a glass of milk or your favorite hot beverage!

Note: Store cookies in an airtight container to maintain freshness.

Peanut Butter and Jelly Thumbprint Cookies

Ingredients:

For the Cookie Dough:

- 1 cup unsalted butter, softened
- 1 cup granulated sugar
- 1 cup creamy peanut butter
- 2 large eggs
- 1 teaspoon vanilla extract
- 2 1/2 cups all-purpose flour
- 1 teaspoon baking powder
- 1/2 teaspoon salt

For the Filling:

- Your favorite fruit jam or jelly (strawberry, raspberry, grape, etc.)

Instructions:

Preheat the oven to 350°F (180°C). Line baking sheets with parchment paper.

In a large bowl, cream together the softened butter, granulated sugar, and peanut butter until light and fluffy. Add the eggs one at a time, beating well after each addition. Stir in the vanilla extract.

In a separate bowl, whisk together the all-purpose flour, baking powder, and salt. Gradually add the dry ingredients to the wet ingredients, mixing until just combined. Shape tablespoon-sized portions of the cookie dough into balls and place them on the prepared baking sheets.

Use your thumb or the back of a spoon to make an indentation in the center of each cookie.

Fill each indentation with a small amount of your favorite fruit jam or jelly.

Bake in the preheated oven for 10-12 minutes or until the edges are set and the cookies are lightly golden.

Allow the cookies to cool on the baking sheets for 5 minutes before transferring them to a wire rack to cool completely.

These Peanut Butter and Jelly Thumbprint Cookies are a classic and nostalgic treat.

Enjoy the timeless combination of peanut butter and fruity jelly in every delicious bite!

Note: Store cookies in an airtight container to maintain freshness.

Snickerdoodle Cookies

Ingredients:

For the Cookie Dough:

- 1 cup unsalted butter, softened
- 1 1/2 cups granulated sugar
- 2 large eggs
- 1 teaspoon vanilla extract
- 2 3/4 cups all-purpose flour
- 1 1/2 teaspoons cream of tartar
- 1/2 teaspoon baking soda
- 1/4 teaspoon salt

For the Cinnamon Sugar Coating:

- 1/4 cup granulated sugar
- 1 tablespoon ground cinnamon

Instructions:

Preheat the oven to 350°F (180°C). Line baking sheets with parchment paper.

In a large bowl, cream together the softened butter and granulated sugar until light and fluffy. Add the eggs one at a time, beating well after each addition. Stir in the vanilla extract.

In a separate bowl, whisk together the all-purpose flour, cream of tartar, baking soda, and salt. Gradually add the dry ingredients to the wet ingredients, mixing until just combined.

In a small bowl, combine the granulated sugar and ground cinnamon for the coating.

Shape tablespoon-sized portions of the cookie dough into balls.

Roll each ball in the cinnamon sugar mixture to coat it completely.

Place the coated cookie dough balls on the prepared baking sheets, spacing them about 2 inches apart.

Bake in the preheated oven for 10-12 minutes or until the edges are set and the cookies are lightly golden.

Allow the cookies to cool on the baking sheets for 5 minutes before transferring them to a wire rack to cool completely.

These Snickerdoodle Cookies are a timeless favorite with their soft and chewy texture and the perfect blend of cinnamon and sugar. Enjoy these classic cookies with a cup of milk or your favorite beverage!

Note: Store cookies in an airtight container to maintain freshness.

Coconut Macaroons

Ingredients:

- 3 cups sweetened shredded coconut
- 3/4 cup sweetened condensed milk
- 1 teaspoon vanilla extract
- 2 large egg whites
- 1/4 teaspoon salt
- Optional: 1 cup chocolate chips (for dipping)

Instructions:

Preheat the oven to 325°F (163°C). Line baking sheets with parchment paper.

In a large bowl, combine the sweetened shredded coconut, sweetened condensed milk, and vanilla extract. Mix well.

In a separate bowl, beat the egg whites with salt until stiff peaks form.

Gently fold the beaten egg whites into the coconut mixture until well combined.

Drop rounded tablespoons of the coconut mixture onto the prepared baking sheets, spacing them about 2 inches apart.

Bake in the preheated oven for 15-20 minutes or until the edges are golden brown.

Allow the coconut macaroons to cool on the baking sheets for 5 minutes before transferring them to a wire rack to cool completely.

Optional: Melt chocolate chips in the microwave or using a double boiler. Dip the bottoms of the cooled macaroons into the melted chocolate and place them on parchment paper to set.

These Coconut Macaroons are chewy on the inside with a crisp exterior. Enjoy the sweet coconut flavor and, if desired, the added indulgence of chocolate!

Note: Store macaroons in an airtight container at room temperature.

White Chocolate Cranberry Cookies

Ingredients:

- 1 cup unsalted butter, softened
- 1 cup granulated sugar
- 2 large eggs
- 1 teaspoon vanilla extract
- 2 1/2 cups all-purpose flour
- 1 teaspoon baking powder
- 1/2 teaspoon baking soda
- 1/4 teaspoon salt
- 1 cup white chocolate chips
- 1 cup dried cranberries

Instructions:

Preheat the oven to 350°F (180°C). Line baking sheets with parchment paper.

In a large bowl, cream together the softened butter and granulated sugar until light and fluffy. Add the eggs one at a time, beating well after each addition. Stir in the vanilla extract.

In a separate bowl, whisk together the all-purpose flour, baking powder, baking soda, and salt. Gradually add the dry ingredients to the wet ingredients, mixing until just combined. Fold in the white chocolate chips and dried cranberries.

Drop rounded tablespoons of cookie dough onto the prepared baking sheets, spacing them about 2 inches apart.

Bake in the preheated oven for 10-12 minutes or until the edges are set and the cookies are lightly golden.

Allow the cookies to cool on the baking sheets for 5 minutes before transferring them to a wire rack to cool completely.

These White Chocolate Cranberry Cookies offer a delightful combination of sweet white chocolate and tart cranberries. Enjoy these festive cookies as a treat during the holidays or any time of the year!

Note: Store cookies in an airtight container to maintain freshness.

Maple Pecan Shortbread Cookies

Ingredients:

For the Cookie Dough:

- 1 cup unsalted butter, softened
- 1/2 cup powdered sugar
- 2 tablespoons pure maple syrup
- 2 cups all-purpose flour
- 1/2 cup chopped pecans

For the Maple Glaze:

- 1 cup powdered sugar
- 2 tablespoons pure maple syrup
- 1-2 tablespoons milk

Instructions:

Preheat the oven to 350°F (180°C). Line baking sheets with parchment paper.

In a large bowl, cream together the softened butter and powdered sugar until light and fluffy. Add the pure maple syrup and mix until well combined.

Gradually add the all-purpose flour to the wet ingredients, mixing until a soft dough forms.

Fold in the chopped pecans.

Divide the dough in half. Shape each portion into a log, approximately 1 1/2 inches in diameter.

Wrap the logs in plastic wrap and chill in the refrigerator for at least 1 hour or until firm.

Slice the chilled logs into 1/4-inch thick rounds and place them on the prepared baking sheets.

Bake in the preheated oven for 12-15 minutes or until the edges are lightly golden.

Allow the shortbread cookies to cool on the baking sheets for 5 minutes before transferring them to a wire rack to cool completely.

In a small bowl, whisk together the powdered sugar, pure maple syrup, and milk to make the maple glaze.

Drizzle the maple glaze over the cooled cookies.

These Maple Pecan Shortbread Cookies are a delightful combination of buttery shortbread, crunchy pecans, and sweet maple glaze. Enjoy these rich and flavorful cookies with a cup of tea or coffee!

Note: Store cookies in an airtight container to maintain freshness.

Lemon Poppy Seed Cookies

Ingredients:

For the Cookie Dough:

- 1 cup unsalted butter, softened
- 1 cup granulated sugar
- Zest of 2 lemons
- 3 tablespoons fresh lemon juice
- 2 large eggs
- 3 cups all-purpose flour
- 1 tablespoon poppy seeds
- 1 teaspoon baking powder
- 1/2 teaspoon baking soda
- 1/4 teaspoon salt

For the Lemon Glaze:

- 1 cup powdered sugar
- 2 tablespoons fresh lemon juice
- Zest of 1 lemon

Instructions:

Preheat the oven to 350°F (180°C). Line baking sheets with parchment paper.

In a large bowl, cream together the softened butter and granulated sugar until light and fluffy. Add the lemon zest, fresh lemon juice, and eggs, mixing well.

In a separate bowl, whisk together the all-purpose flour, poppy seeds, baking powder, baking soda, and salt. Gradually add the dry ingredients to the wet ingredients, mixing until just combined.

Drop rounded tablespoons of cookie dough onto the prepared baking sheets, spacing them about 2 inches apart.

Bake in the preheated oven for 10-12 minutes or until the edges are set and the cookies are lightly golden.

Allow the cookies to cool on the baking sheets for 5 minutes before transferring them to a wire rack to cool completely.

In a small bowl, whisk together the powdered sugar, fresh lemon juice, and lemon zest to make the lemon glaze.

Drizzle the lemon glaze over the cooled cookies.

These Lemon Poppy Seed Cookies offer a burst of citrusy flavor and a delightful crunch from the poppy seeds. Enjoy these light and refreshing cookies with a cup of tea or as a sweet treat!

Note: Store cookies in an airtight container to maintain freshness.

Caramel Pecan Chocolate Thumbprint Cookies

Ingredients:

For the Cookie Dough:

- 1 cup unsalted butter, softened
- 1/2 cup granulated sugar
- 2 large egg yolks
- 2 teaspoons vanilla extract
- 2 cups all-purpose flour
- 1/2 teaspoon salt

For the Filling:

- 1 cup caramel candies, unwrapped
- 2 tablespoons heavy cream
- 1 cup chopped pecans, toasted

For Drizzling (optional):

- 1/2 cup chocolate chips, melted

Instructions:

Preheat the oven to 350°F (180°C). Line baking sheets with parchment paper.

In a large bowl, cream together the softened butter and granulated sugar until light and fluffy. Add the egg yolks and vanilla extract, beating well.

In a separate bowl, whisk together the all-purpose flour and salt. Gradually add the dry ingredients to the wet ingredients, mixing until just combined.

Shape tablespoon-sized portions of the cookie dough into balls and place them on the prepared baking sheets.

Make an indentation in the center of each cookie with your thumb or the back of a spoon.

In a small saucepan, melt the caramel candies with the heavy cream over low heat, stirring until smooth.

Spoon a small amount of the caramel filling into the indentation of each cookie.

Sprinkle toasted chopped pecans over the caramel filling.

Bake in the preheated oven for 10-12 minutes or until the edges are set and the cookies are lightly golden.

Allow the cookies to cool on the baking sheets for 5 minutes before transferring them to a wire rack to cool completely.

Optional: Melt chocolate chips and drizzle over the cooled cookies for an extra touch.

These Caramel Pecan Chocolate Thumbprint Cookies are a delightful combination of buttery cookies, gooey caramel, and crunchy pecans. Enjoy the rich flavors of caramel and chocolate in every delicious bite!

Note: Store cookies in an airtight container to maintain freshness.

Chai Spice Snickerdoodle Cookies

Ingredients:

For the Cookie Dough:

- 1 cup unsalted butter, softened
- 1 1/2 cups granulated sugar
- 2 large eggs
- 1 teaspoon vanilla extract
- 3 cups all-purpose flour
- 1 teaspoon cream of tartar
- 1/2 teaspoon baking soda
- 1/4 teaspoon salt

For the Chai Spice Coating:

- 1/4 cup granulated sugar
- 1 teaspoon ground cinnamon
- 1/2 teaspoon ground ginger
- 1/2 teaspoon ground cardamom
- 1/4 teaspoon ground cloves
- 1/4 teaspoon ground nutmeg

Instructions:

Preheat the oven to 350°F (180°C). Line baking sheets with parchment paper.
In a large bowl, cream together the softened butter and granulated sugar until light and fluffy. Add the eggs one at a time, beating well after each addition. Stir in the vanilla extract.
In a separate bowl, whisk together the all-purpose flour, cream of tartar, baking soda, and salt. Gradually add the dry ingredients to the wet ingredients, mixing until just combined.
In a small bowl, combine the granulated sugar, ground cinnamon, ground ginger, ground cardamom, ground cloves, and ground nutmeg for the chai spice coating.
Shape tablespoon-sized portions of the cookie dough into balls.
Roll each ball in the chai spice coating mixture to coat it completely.
Place the coated cookie dough balls on the prepared baking sheets, spacing them about 2 inches apart.

Bake in the preheated oven for 10-12 minutes or until the edges are set and the cookies are lightly golden.

Allow the cookies to cool on the baking sheets for 5 minutes before transferring them to a wire rack to cool completely.

These Chai Spice Snickerdoodle Cookies offer a warm and aromatic twist to the classic snickerdoodle. Enjoy the cozy flavors of chai spices in every delightful bite!

Note: Store cookies in an airtight container to maintain freshness.

Pistachio Cranberry Biscotti

Ingredients:

- 2 cups all-purpose flour
- 1 cup granulated sugar
- 1 teaspoon baking powder
- 1/4 teaspoon salt
- 3 large eggs
- 1 teaspoon vanilla extract
- 1 cup shelled pistachios, chopped
- 1 cup dried cranberries

Instructions:

Preheat the oven to 350°F (180°C). Line a baking sheet with parchment paper.
In a large bowl, whisk together the all-purpose flour, granulated sugar, baking powder, and salt.
In a separate bowl, beat the eggs and vanilla extract until well combined.
Gradually add the egg mixture to the dry ingredients, mixing until a dough forms.
Fold in the chopped pistachios and dried cranberries until evenly distributed.
Divide the dough in half and shape each portion into a log, about 12 inches long and 2 inches wide.
Place the logs on the prepared baking sheet, leaving space between them.
Bake in the preheated oven for 25-30 minutes or until the logs are set and lightly golden.
Allow the logs to cool on the baking sheet for 10 minutes.
Using a sharp knife, slice the logs into 1/2-inch wide biscotti.
Place the biscotti back on the baking sheet, cut side down, and bake for an additional 10-15 minutes or until they are crisp and golden.
Allow the biscotti to cool completely before serving.
These Pistachio Cranberry Biscotti are perfect for dipping in coffee or tea. Enjoy the combination of crunchy pistachios and tart cranberries in this delightful twice-baked treat!

Note: Store biscotti in an airtight container to maintain crispiness.

Raspberry Almond Thumbprint Cookies

Ingredients:

For the Cookie Dough:

- 1 cup unsalted butter, softened
- 2/3 cup granulated sugar
- 1/2 teaspoon almond extract
- 2 cups all-purpose flour
- 1/2 cup almond flour
- 1/4 teaspoon salt

For the Filling:

- Raspberry jam or preserves

For Garnish:

- Sliced almonds

Instructions:

Preheat the oven to 350°F (180°C). Line baking sheets with parchment paper.
In a large bowl, cream together the softened butter and granulated sugar until light and fluffy. Add the almond extract and mix well.
In a separate bowl, whisk together the all-purpose flour, almond flour, and salt. Gradually add the dry ingredients to the wet ingredients, mixing until just combined.
Shape tablespoon-sized portions of the cookie dough into balls and place them on the prepared baking sheets.
Make an indentation in the center of each cookie with your thumb or the back of a spoon.
Fill each indentation with a small amount of raspberry jam or preserves.
Garnish each cookie with sliced almonds.
Bake in the preheated oven for 12-15 minutes or until the edges are set and the cookies are lightly golden.
Allow the cookies to cool on the baking sheets for 5 minutes before transferring them to a wire rack to cool completely.
These Raspberry Almond Thumbprint Cookies are a delightful blend of buttery almond-flavored cookies and sweet raspberry filling. Enjoy these tender and flavorful cookies with a cup of tea or as a special treat!

Note: Store cookies in an airtight container to maintain freshness.

Coconut Lime Sugar Cookies

Ingredients:

For the Cookie Dough:

- 1 cup unsalted butter, softened
- 1 cup granulated sugar
- 2 large eggs
- 1 teaspoon vanilla extract
- Zest of 2 limes
- 3 cups all-purpose flour
- 1/2 teaspoon baking powder
- 1/4 teaspoon salt

For Rolling:

- 1/2 cup sweetened shredded coconut
- Additional granulated sugar for rolling

Instructions:

Preheat the oven to 350°F (180°C). Line baking sheets with parchment paper.
In a large bowl, cream together the softened butter and granulated sugar until light and fluffy. Add the eggs one at a time, beating well after each addition. Stir in the vanilla extract and lime zest.
In a separate bowl, whisk together the all-purpose flour, baking powder, and salt.
Gradually add the dry ingredients to the wet ingredients, mixing until just combined.
Shape tablespoon-sized portions of the cookie dough into balls.
In a small bowl, combine sweetened shredded coconut with additional granulated sugar.
Roll each cookie dough ball in the coconut and sugar mixture to coat it completely.
Place the coated cookie dough balls on the prepared baking sheets, spacing them about 2 inches apart.
Flatten each cookie slightly with the back of a spoon or your fingers.
Bake in the preheated oven for 10-12 minutes or until the edges are set and the cookies are lightly golden.
Allow the cookies to cool on the baking sheets for 5 minutes before transferring them to a wire rack to cool completely.
These Coconut Lime Sugar Cookies offer a tropical twist with the refreshing flavors of lime and coconut. Enjoy these zesty and sweet cookies as a delightful treat!

Note: Store cookies in an airtight container to maintain freshness.

Chocolate Mint Sandwich Cookies

Ingredients:

For the Chocolate Cookies:

- 1 cup unsalted butter, softened
- 1 cup granulated sugar
- 2 large eggs
- 1 teaspoon vanilla extract
- 2 cups all-purpose flour
- 1/2 cup unsweetened cocoa powder
- 1/2 teaspoon baking powder
- 1/4 teaspoon salt

For the Mint Filling:

- 1/2 cup unsalted butter, softened
- 2 cups powdered sugar
- 1/2 teaspoon peppermint extract
- Green food coloring (optional)
- Chocolate chips for decoration (optional)

Instructions:

Preheat the oven to 350°F (180°C). Line baking sheets with parchment paper.
In a large bowl, cream together the softened butter and granulated sugar until light and fluffy. Add the eggs one at a time, beating well after each addition. Stir in the vanilla extract.
In a separate bowl, whisk together the all-purpose flour, cocoa powder, baking powder, and salt. Gradually add the dry ingredients to the wet ingredients, mixing until just combined.
Shape tablespoon-sized portions of the cookie dough into balls and place them on the prepared baking sheets.
Flatten each cookie slightly with the back of a spoon or your fingers.
Bake in the preheated oven for 10-12 minutes or until the edges are set and the cookies are slightly firm.

Allow the cookies to cool on the baking sheets for 5 minutes before transferring them to a wire rack to cool completely.

In a separate bowl, prepare the mint filling by creaming together the softened butter, powdered sugar, peppermint extract, and green food coloring (if using).

Once the cookies are completely cooled, spread a layer of mint filling on the bottom side of half of the cookies.

Top each filled cookie with another cookie, creating sandwich cookies.

Optional: Melt chocolate chips and drizzle over the top of the sandwich cookies for decoration.

These Chocolate Mint Sandwich Cookies are a delightful combination of rich chocolate cookies and cool mint filling. Enjoy these festive cookies as a treat for any occasion!

Note: Store cookies in an airtight container to maintain freshness.

Lemon Blueberry Cheesecake Cookies

Ingredients:

For the Cookie Dough:

- 1 cup unsalted butter, softened
- 1 cup granulated sugar
- Zest of 2 lemons
- 2 large eggs
- 1 teaspoon vanilla extract
- 3 cups all-purpose flour
- 1/2 teaspoon baking soda
- 1/2 teaspoon baking powder
- 1/4 teaspoon salt

For the Blueberry Cheesecake Filling:

- 4 ounces cream cheesc, softened
- 1/4 cup granulated sugar
- 1 large egg
- 1/2 cup fresh blueberries

Instructions:

Preheat the oven to 350°F (180°C). Line baking sheets with parchment paper.
In a large bowl, cream together the softened butter and granulated sugar until light and fluffy. Add the lemon zest, eggs, and vanilla extract, mixing well.
In a separate bowl, whisk together the all-purpose flour, baking soda, baking powder, and salt. Gradually add the dry ingredients to the wet ingredients, mixing until just combined.
In another bowl, prepare the blueberry cheesecake filling by beating together the softened cream cheese, sugar, and egg until smooth. Fold in the fresh blueberries.
Shape tablespoon-sized portions of the cookie dough into balls and place them on the prepared baking sheets.
Flatten each cookie slightly and make an indentation in the center with your thumb or the back of a spoon.
Spoon a small amount of the blueberry cheesecake filling into the indentation of each cookie.
Bake in the preheated oven for 12-15 minutes or until the edges are set and the cookies are lightly golden.

Allow the cookies to cool on the baking sheets for 5 minutes before transferring them to a wire rack to cool completely.

These Lemon Blueberry Cheesecake Cookies combine the bright citrus flavor of lemon with the sweetness of blueberry cheesecake. Enjoy these fruity and creamy cookies as a delightful treat!

Note: Store cookies in an airtight container to maintain freshness.

Pumpkin Spice Chocolate Chip Cookies

Ingredients:

For the Cookie Dough:

- 1 cup unsalted butter, softened
- 1 cup granulated sugar
- 1 cup canned pumpkin puree
- 1 large egg
- 1 teaspoon vanilla extract
- 3 cups all-purpose flour
- 1 teaspoon baking powder
- 1/2 teaspoon baking soda
- 1/2 teaspoon salt
- 1 teaspoon ground cinnamon
- 1/2 teaspoon ground nutmeg
- 1/2 teaspoon ground ginger
- 1/4 teaspoon ground cloves
- 1 cup chocolate chips

Instructions:

Preheat the oven to 350°F (180°C). Line baking sheets with parchment paper.
In a large bowl, cream together the softened butter and granulated sugar until light and fluffy. Add the pumpkin puree, egg, and vanilla extract, mixing well.
In a separate bowl, whisk together the all-purpose flour, baking powder, baking soda, salt, cinnamon, nutmeg, ginger, and cloves. Gradually add the dry ingredients to the wet ingredients, mixing until just combined.
Fold in the chocolate chips.
Drop rounded tablespoons of cookie dough onto the prepared baking sheets, spacing them about 2 inches apart.
Bake in the preheated oven for 12-15 minutes or until the edges are set and the cookies are lightly golden.
Allow the cookies to cool on the baking sheets for 5 minutes before transferring them to a wire rack to cool completely.
These Pumpkin Spice Chocolate Chip Cookies are a perfect fall treat, combining the warmth of pumpkin spice with the sweetness of chocolate chips. Enjoy these flavorful and festive cookies with a cup of your favorite warm beverage!

Note: Store cookies in an airtight container to maintain freshness.

Salted Caramel Pecan Cookies

Ingredients:

For the Cookie Dough:

- 1 cup unsalted butter, softened
- 1 cup granulated sugar
- 2 large eggs
- 1 teaspoon vanilla extract
- 2 cups all-purpose flour
- 1/2 teaspoon baking soda
- 1/4 teaspoon salt
- 1 cup chopped pecans

For the Salted Caramel Drizzle:

- 1/2 cup caramel sauce (store-bought or homemade)
- Flaky sea salt for sprinkling

Instructions:

Preheat the oven to 350°F (180°C). Line baking sheets with parchment paper.
In a large bowl, cream together the softened butter and granulated sugar until light and fluffy. Add the eggs and vanilla extract, mixing well.
In a separate bowl, whisk together the all-purpose flour, baking soda, and salt. Gradually add the dry ingredients to the wet ingredients, mixing until just combined.
Fold in the chopped pecans.
Drop rounded tablespoons of cookie dough onto the prepared baking sheets, spacing them about 2 inches apart.
Bake in the preheated oven for 10-12 minutes or until the edges are set and the cookies are lightly golden.
Allow the cookies to cool on the baking sheets for 5 minutes before transferring them to a wire rack to cool completely.
In a small saucepan, warm the caramel sauce over low heat until it's pourable.
Drizzle each cooled cookie with salted caramel and sprinkle with flaky sea salt.
These Salted Caramel Pecan Cookies offer a perfect balance of sweet and salty flavors. Enjoy the buttery pecans and rich caramel drizzle in every delightful bite!

Note: Store cookies in an airtight container to maintain freshness.